Something About Faith

Observing God's Move

By

Anne M. Scott

Watersprings
PUBLISHING

Published by Watersprings Publishing a division of
Watersprings Media House, LLC.
P.O. BOX 1284
Olive Branch, MS 38654
www.waterspringsmedia.com
Contact publisher for bulk orders and permission requests.

Library of Congress Control Number: 2019919297

Printed in the United States of America.

ISBN-13:   978-1-94877-30-5

I would like to dedicate this book to my mother Dalma Dougherty. She has been there through my travels in the military, she listened to my calls each time I experienced my faith moments and gave me guidance along the way.

Table of Contents

Foreword

What is faith? It is the confident assurance that something we want is going to happen. It is the certainty that what we hope for is waiting for us, even though we cannot see it up ahead. (Hebrews 11:1 TLB)

Faith is a term that we have defined on our own terms. We attribute great faith to ease, and a lack of faith to uncertainty. We also look at faith based on what we perceive to be true with our natural eyes versus through the eyes of faith. *Something About Faith* reminds us that God is a very present help in trouble as well as in triumph.

Hebrews 11:1 reminds us that faith is "confident assurance" that we will experience the promises we are entitled to as children of God. 1 John 5:14 gives further assurance of faith by reminding us that when we ask according to His will, we are heard. *Something About Faith* helps us to navigate the journey of unanswered prayers and requests to embracing God's promises in various facets of our pilgrimage. It is a book that will help you to present each request to God with the assurance that you are heard.

Observing the example of Ms. Scott, this message is one she not only writes about, but lives. Her dependence and belief in God are compelling. Having the joy of hearing how God made His presence known in her life and her family's brought fresh strength to my life in some challenging moments. I know that this book will ignite your faith and renew your strength in pursuing God and His promises. Prepare for a fresh encounter with God in your daily life as you absorb the wisdom contained in each page and prompt. As you read this book, you will grow from a surface knowledge of faith to a deep, rich understanding of its relevance in your daily life.

Ashley Sauls,

Author of Morning Motivation

1

Something About Faith

And Jesus said to the woman, "Your faith has saved you; go in peace." Luke 7:50 NIV

When you pray and believe God for what you prayed, you have to make the first step to get the wheels of faith moving. In the Bible days experiencing answered prayer was the norm. People would pray and knew there would be an answer in some form. Today, I think we are praying with doubt and not faith. I think we pray with some form of faith, but not totally hand over what it is we are trusting Him for. We often hold on to it and try to work on it ourselves. Sometimes we end up with bad outcomes due to us doing the work and not allowing God to do His work.

For me, my experience of asking God for things started at a very young age, and seeing how God delivered caused me to be more aware of God's goodness and what He can do for me. As I got older and started to know the scriptures, I realized there was power in those scriptures. Once I started memorizing them, I also started to put them into action. One of my favorite scriptures is Hebrews 11:1, *"Now faith is the substance of things hoped for and the evidence of things not seen"*. With that, always remember that faith without works is dead (James 2:26 KJV). You can't believe God will give you a job and not apply for one. Sometimes when we start off on our faith journey, whatever that may be, we sometimes head in the wrong direction, but the point is you making that first step. Many first steps are difficult. There are a lot of uncertainties, twists and turns, but we should not give up.

When you pray for something, move towards it, put in the work. Don't just sit there and wait for God to bring it to you. He may not answer that prayer in the way you'd expect, but the important thing is working alongside God to reach His plans for you. Once on the path, you may find obstacles, but they are there to help you, and strengthen you. How can our faith be strengthened if we do not stay the course?

Some days, while in the faith process, you may want to give up, throw in the towel, but if you anchor your mustard seed of faith (Matthew 17:20) and have patience, God will come through for you. I am a living witness to that. There were many times I wanted to give up on something I prayed for and there wasn't a "right now" delivery. One of those moments was when I prayed for a house in Texas and it took 10 years to get it. The wait was long, but during that waiting period I was traveling the world and each move from one place to another was Him working strategically to bring me to that place; wanting all of my kids to be at home at the same time, it took over a year.

I know God is an on-time God. I have learned that I have to have patience in the process. Sometimes I tried to give God a hand with what I asked for and that did not work out. When we try to help God, we oftentimes delay what we are believing Him for. We don't often have the patience it takes to allow our faith to work. Always remember God is an on-time God. He will be there when you need Him, just trust Him and have patience.

I would like you to take these faith moments I am sharing with you to help encourage you along the way. You will be prompted to write your experience down and reflect on how God is working in your life, some of the things you have prayed for, and how He answered your prayer.

In your life, when have you waited for God to answer your prayers without acting? When have you tried to take God's plan for you in your own hands? Did that work out well for you?

2

Healed by Faith

When this man heard that Jesus had arrived in Galilee from Judea, he went to him and begged him to come and heal his son, who was close.   "Unless you people see signs and wonders," Jesus told him, "you will never believe." The royal official said, "Sir, come down before my child dies."

"Go," Jesus replied, "your son will live."   The man took Jesus at his word and departed. While he was still on the way, his servants met him with the news that his boy was living. When he inquired as to the time when his son got better, they said to him, "Yesterday, at one in the afternoon, the fever left him."   Then the father realized that this was the exact time at which Jesus had said to him, "Your son will live." So he and his whole household believed.

John 4:47-53 NIV

While living in Jamaica at about the age of six or seven I remember one Saturday morning I got very sick and needed to go to the doctor. I was having problems breathing and my foster mom became very worried. Back then we did not have the luxury of a car, and calling 911 was not an option either.

My uncle, who was staying with us at the time, had to walk quite a few miles to get a taxi from the main road so that I could get to the doctor. We lived in Rose Hall, Linstead an area in St. Catherine that was not really the "country" but neither was it the "town/city". Very few people had a car, so we mostly walked to the main street to get public transportation to get where we were going. I am not sure how many miles we had to walk, but it was quite a distance.

While he was out looking for a taxi, me and my mummy waited in the living room listening to the radio. We had an old Grundig stereo, one with a record player on the bottom and a radio on top. Oral Roberts, who was a prominent preacher on the radio back then, was about to pray. Every time he would say, "place your hand on the radio" so that he could pray for you.

My mummy (the lady who raised me) lifted me up and sat me on top of the radio. This was her faith in action. She was believing for my healing no matter what the natural outcome would look like. At that age I was not thinking about what would happen. I was not sure of the working of God and what He could do. It was years later that I realized what God had done that day. As I remember what had taken place that day, I then knew that God was real and if He did that for me that day, He could do much more in my life and for others. Oral Roberts prayed, and I was feeling better not long after he prayed. I did not know what healing was at that age. I was up and about the rest of the day and don't remember if my uncle ever showed up with the taxi. Mummy placed her faith in God that He would heal me, and He did. Her faith made her stronger in Him.

In the Bible, they spoke of Jesus healing others without even being in their presence. You don't need to have Him lay hands on you, touch His robe, or even a holy relic. Healing is the result of having faith that it will be done.

Because of my healing, I have never doubted God about anything. This episode of faith in action gave me all that I needed to live my life. Once I realized God's goodness, I started to place every aspect of my life in His hands. Yes, there are times I get impatient and want things right away. That is when I have to remind myself that God is working on it and it will come right on time. I know God can do anything, and if we ask in faith and believe that He will come through, He will.

In the past they had tried old wives' tale remedies, like chopping down papaya trees over my head or anointing my head with various oils to cure what ailed me. But none of those were more powerful than God's healing and His sustaining force. My breathing issue was asthma, I often had attacks and had to go to the hospital to get treatment.

Are you in need of healing? Healing of the body? Healing in the mind? He did it for me, He can do it for you.

Ask God to heal your ailments and have faith that He will answer your prayers.

3

Seeing the World by Faith

A man's heart deviseth his way: but the LORD directeth his steps.

Proverbs 16:9 KJV

In my lifetime, I have experienced many faith moments. These faith moments would come once I made my request known, then somewhere along the way I would receive what was asked for. Sometimes it may take days, and at other times it may even take years. Many of these moments have guided my life throughout the years. I have found that without faith it is impossible to please God. (Hebrews 11:6).

As a little girl I experienced moments such as my neighbor's dad traveling to the United States and bringing back some really colorful toys, building blocks, and toy trucks that fascinated me. This may seem simple, but to me it was not. The colors were vibrant, the reds, the blues and the yellows. I had never seen anything like that before. This really intrigued me, and I asked him where he got the toys, he said Colorado.

I would often dream of seeing these colors in the place where he got them. At that moment Colorado was on my mind and the thought of how I could get there. I never thought about the distance, because at that age air travel never crossed my mind. My concept of travel was traveling by bus or train from one end of the island to another. I figured I could get to Colorado the same way, little did I know it was much more than that. I started dreaming about the place when a light bulb went off in my head and I said, "I want to go to Colorado." My idea of Colorado at that time was mainly the colorful toys. I had no concept of anything else at that age. At the time, I was nine years old. Who would have thought that a small girl's wish from a small town in Jamaica would actually come true?

You never know how far your faith and dreams will take you when you believe. Your words are powerful, and they can either make you or break you. As time went on and my request was made, the God I know and serve started working it out. During this time while the years were going by, I was healed of asthma, I had to move to live with my mom because mummy was sick and then she eventually died. My mother then started having conversations with my grandmother who was living in the United States, for me to migrate and live with her. Experiencing these changes was not easy. I had lost the person I knew as mother, although I had my biological mother. Can you see the elements in motion to get me to my nine-year-old self's request? I imagined the various parts of a clock turning to move the hands to give the correct time, and yes, those parts were in motion for me.

Over seven years later, at the age of 18 while living with my father in California, I decided to join the United States Army. My father was in the Army and his job at the time was to recruit soldiers for the military. I used to travel with him at times when he was taking his recruits to drop them off at their first stop on their military journey. I was fascinated by the uniforms and asked my dad if I could join. He told me no, because I would cry and would want to come home. I kept pressuring my dad about joining and he finally gave in. He became my recruiter.

Once I passed all my tests, it was time to pick the job path I qualified for and the one I chose led me to my very first duty station. After my basic training in South Carolina my first duty station was—yes, you guessed it—Colorado. Yes, that nine-year-old request was answered in spite of the distance between the place of request and the place of prayer answered. Ask, and ye shall receive (Luke 11:9). Who would have thought!

I learned a lot from my neighbors, and every now and then there is that one who seemed a little off. There was Victor who was a self-proclaimed magician. He would do all sorts of tricks with threads and other things. One day he was doing his tricks and then asked me to participate by holding out my hand. After surveying my hand, he told me that I would travel the world. His magic was not the cause of my traveling the world, it was the thought that such a thing could happen and me believing God for it to happen. It was one of those moments where you think that there was more out there beyond the island I lived on and imagining the possibilities of such a thing.

My brain started working and I started to imagine the world that I would travel. I am not sure how he came up with that, but I took it and filed it away in my little nine-year-old mind. The world that I knew back then in Jamaica was leaving the countryside and traveling to the main town, Kingston.

When I had to leave to live with my mother, I thought I had "traveled." I guess that was the first leg of my world travels. The reason for me not living with my mother was because she needed help raising me and mummy took me in so that she could attend school and get a job. My mother was 19 when she had me.

I have indeed traveled the world thanks to Uncle Sam. I enlisted in the military in 1980. My father was also in the military and he was my reluctant recruiter. My father eventually signed the papers for me to enlist. I have been to places I often saw on TV. I witnessed history, watching the Berlin Wall coming down. Stood at General Patten's grave in Luxembourg. Crossed the border into East Germany and experienced how foreigners were treated, as if we were in a spy movie. Shopped in Czechoslovakia, drove through the deserts of Saudi Arabia, visited the salt mines in Austria and the place where the Sound of Music was made.

My little nine-year-old mind could not have dreamed all that. It was in the asking that that nine-year-old girl ignited that mustard seed of faith, not knowing that years later the world would be her playground.

What are you trusting God for?

How far will you stretch your faith?

4

Trusting God in The Midst of Uncertainty

Trust in the LORD with all thine heart; and lean not unto thine own understanding. In all thy ways acknowledge him, and he shall direct thy paths.

Prov 3:5-6 KJV

In 1990 about nine or ten years after being stationed in Colorado, I was stationed in Germany, a place I so loved. I loved the culture, the language, and its people. I lived in a community where hardly anyone spoke English, so I had to learn the language and how to communicate to my landlord who was Polish. While there, I wanted my mom to come and visit. She had visited me before while I was stationed in Panama, but this visit would be quite different. I wanted my mom to stay. I did not know how I would pull it off financially. I had to save money for her flight to get her there. I also wanted her to return with me back to the United States. I had tried for years to have her visit me in the United States, but she was always denied. I started trying to figure out how she would be able to come back with me. I knew it was bigger than me, so I had to leave it in God's hand.

During one of our many conversations, I told her to bring all her important documents with her. She wondered what I was up to. We made the plans, bought the ticket and the wheels were in motion. The day my mom landed in Frankfurt, Germany she just walked right out the airport without being checked (a bit strange, I would have thought immigration would check her documents). Once she was settled, I decided to make her my military dependent because she was living with me (no hitch to that). While my mom was living with me in Germany, she helped with the children when I was at work. We also attended an American church while being there. My husband and I were both in the military and her being there took some of the stress off us when working long hours.

One particular Friday, I was prompted to go to the Embassy in Frankfurt to start working on her document to grant her permission to enter the United States.

Sometimes I get these feelings where I am prompted to do something like that and have to follow through. I was living in Hanau at the time, which was about a half hour or so from Frankfurt. I had planned to drive up early in the afternoon to take care of the visa application, but I didn't realize the offices took a half-day on Fridays. Luckily, I arrived an hour before the embassy closed for the weekend.

The lady who took care of us was very nice and was very willing to help us, she looked everything over and told me I was missing one thing. I had to drive back to Hanau to get it—an hour total for the trip. She told me she would wait until I returned and when I do, I should tell the guard at the gate I was there to see her (in other cases they would have me to come back another day). I drove home, collected the document, and proceeded back to Frankfurt. Once I returned, we engaged in a conversation. In the course of the conversation, I learned that she had just lost her mother. She told me to always take care of my mother and do all I could for her.

Everything was approved in one day.

How awesome that is, that a process that would take weeks was resolved in a day? God was in the midst the whole time.

Unbeknownst to me, there was a war coming, and I was to be deployed to Iraq. I had three small kids. At first, it seemed as if my husband was the one who was going to be deployed, but it ended up being me. This happened three months after my mother got to Germany (if you listen to His voice, you will never go wrong).

I got all mom's military documents squared away and set things up should I not return, so she would be able to take my kids to the United States. I tried leaving my husband in charge of things, but he kept saying he did not want to talk about it (the what ifs). I had to make a decision fast because Uncle Sam was not going to change his mind. I turned over my bank account to my mother, bills and all. I had an angry spouse, but the clock was ticking.

My husband at the time was scheduled to deploy, so we were already preparing for him to leave, and during that process is when I found out that I was leaving. I was feeling nervous that both of us were about to deploy and leave the kids with mom. My husband started panicking about what was happening and could not make coherent decisions, so I had to plan for my mom to be in charge. His orders eventually got cancelled from deploying the same time I was.

It was right before Christmas when I had to board the bus heading to the airport. At the time of my deployment we were residing in a German community quite a distance away from the military base. Once I boarded the bus, my husband left the house and moved into the barracks leaving my mother and the kids in a German neighborhood, not knowing the language and without transportation—but God! During this time, I could not stress over what I had no control over. I had to place it all in God's hand and trust that He would work it all out. Yes, I was upset when I first got the news of him leaving the home, but I had to rely on God to help my mom. God worked it out so that people would pick her and the kids up, take them to the store, and to church. God was in it the whole time. He saw her through that rough time.

Thank God for a short war and for sparing my life through it all. I was one of the very first ones from my unit to make it back home.

I would like you to reflect on a time when you thought God's timing was a bit long and how He finally came through for you.

What wars do you have going on in your life?

5

Asking God for a House in Texas

Oh how great is thy goodness, which thou hast laid up for them that fear thee; which thou has wrought for them that trust in thee before the sons of men! For thou art my rock and my fortress; therefore for thy name's sake lead me, and guide me.

Psalms 31:19 KJV

While in the military and preparing for one of many duty station rotations, I was on my way out from Fort Bliss, located in El Paso, Texas. It was 1984, and duty called me to Panama. After spending a year in El Paso I fell in love with Texas and wanted to live there. It was a Thursday night, and the sky was a little overcast, I was not sure if I would enjoy my upcoming transition. As I observed the sky, I decided to put in my request. I looked up to the heavens and asked God with much expectation for a house in Texas. This was a big order to fill, but I have realized that I serve a BIG God. Texas is a large state and it could be anywhere in Texas. My request was made known (Phil 4:6).

As the years went by and I was busy crossing the world serving in the military I did not remember some of my requests I made unto God. I figured my Father, my heavenly Father owns everything (Psalms 50:10) and anything I need, I could ask Him for it. I went to Panama for three years, then on to Fort Lewis, Washington, Germany and then Fort Polk, Louisiana. Lots of years had passed and God was working it out. While in Fort Polk, my husband received orders for Fort Hood, Texas (faith in process). When this happened, I suddenly remembered my prayer on that Thursday night.

My unit on the other hand did not want to release me. They claimed that they would be shooting themselves in the foot if they released me (the devil trying to block my request "smile"), so they tried to get my husband transferred from his moving unit to one that was not going anywhere. I was upset at the back and forth that was taking place. I was praying for it to all work out. God had it under control in spite of the obstacle being thrown in to prevent my request being answered. I continued to do my duties and remembered that I had prayed years ago for a house in Texas. My request was now shaping up to be a reality. Prayer in motion I would say.

Sometimes we need to be specific when we pray.

My Sergeant Major was the person blocking my request for that house in Texas at the time (kinda shakes your faith a little). There was that thing that awakened in me, reminding me who I am and whose I am. I would say I had to encourage myself, often referring back to Hebrews 11:1. After a short while, the Sergeant Major left the unit and now my husband was free to go with his unit, and I was too.

Things started to shape up. I found a realtor and gave my husband the information so that he could go to Texas and find us a home. Sometimes men don't follow instructions very well. I had secured a realtor ahead of time and told him to contact this place when he arrived in Texas. He did not like the realtor I provided and started looked for another one. The one he got told him that we could not afford the houses we were looking at. I told him to go back to the person I picked and let him help. Not only did we find a home, but we got money back from using the realtor I chose. When we moved in it was ten years to the day I had made my request known. I started to cry, and my husband asked what was wrong and I told him he would not understand. He would not understand that my conversations with God had led to us obtaining a house in Texas. He would not understand because he did not have a relationship with God that would allow him to know how God works, that He was real and working the process out.

When he divorced me, he told me to sell the house. I knew God had answered my prayer from years ago and I figured if He gave it to me, He would allow me to keep it. Nineteen years later, He is still keeping me. Like the Bible says, "faith without works is dead (James 2:20)" and I had to put in the work. I was working three jobs cleaning office buildings, taking care of physically challenged folks on the weekends, and my regular nine to five. Basically, I was working seven days a week.

Along that journey I started to get tired of working seven days a week and I called on my Father, Heavenly Father that is, and asked for help in reducing at least one of the jobs. I waited patiently, and one day my nine to five boss called me in to tell me I was getting a promotion, so I dropped one job. Later on, down the road, things were getting hectic and I started getting tired again and I called on Him for relief and He made it happen again. He answered my prayers once again. He has never failed me. He is keeping me from day to day.

Will you allow Him to keep you?

6

Trusting God to Make a Way

He replied, "Because you have faith. Truly I tell you, if you have faith as small as a mustard seed, you can say to this mountain, 'Move from here to there,' and it will move. Nothing will be impossible for you."

Matt 17:20 NIV

The day after my husband finalized the divorce, I was in a car accident. I had my youngest daughter in modeling and she had a casting call in Dallas. We were on our way back when we were hit from behind by a van. This accident totaled my car. We were a little banged up but we were okay.

I had no money to get another car and had to put everything in God's hands. I had no additional income due to the recent divorce. I had to have transportation to go to work and take the kids to their various events. At this time, I was a civilian working at the hospital. The pay was not enough to take care of such an emergency. I figured this was a good time to test my faith in God.

While at home recuperating from the accident, I started thinking about how I was going to get to work and how the kids were going to get to where they needed to be. I had the only transportation for the family, and now that was no more. I could only think of my true source for everything—God.

At times in my life I get prompted to do different things, this is something that I cannot explain. Maybe I should have went to church and asked for assistance, but the promptings that I got was not in that direction. So without giving it a second thought I walked into the car dealership, exercising my mustard seed faith I told the salesman in this order: my husband just left me, I got into an accident, (I think I said I had no money) my car is totaled, and I need a car. The salesman told me to go to the lot and pick out what I wanted.

I felt like my heavenly Father was speaking. Child, go and pick out what you need.

I figured I was in a small car at the time of the accident, so I was going to get me something much bigger than what I had, a van. A van was much safer, and I later realized it worked out well for transporting all of my family when they visited.

Walking through the lot, I had no fear. I did not stress about the price nor how I was going to pay for it. I totally placed my faith in Him, knowing He would guide me in the right direction. I knew God was in charge and He would direct my path through this transaction. Here comes the most amazing thing of this experience. The salesman drove the van to my house without me doing any paperwork nor having paid a down payment. Yes, he did. He told me whenever I am ready, I could come in and fill out the paperwork.

Although I was operating in faith, I was so overwhelmed of how God came through for me. I could not help but weep like a baby that day, because I had never seen a dealership let you leave without a down payment nor documentation for their vehicles. Often times you have to leave your license so that they can keep track of who has their equipment.

In my weeping state, I called my mother who was living in New York and told her about my experience. I always call her and share all my God moments. I just sat on the floor bawling on the phone, tears of joy and tears of thankfulness. This just affirmed that God was still working in my life.

After my experience, I ran into my neighbor who needed a car herself. I was so excited about what had happened to me and told her about my experience. I figured since she was a believer, she would exercise her faith and that the same thing would happen to her. I actually took her to the lot where I got the car. After walking the lot and talking to her, I realized that her measure of faith (Romans 12:3) was far different from mine.

We left the lot without her getting a vehicle. In that moment, I thought that the same thing that happened to me would also happen to her. My heavenly Father owns everything, and I figure we say that all the time, so why not put it in action? For those of us who do not experience a "yes" the moment we ask, I would encourage you to continue trusting God for what it is you are asking. Request delayed does not mean request denied.

How have you seen God bless you for your unwavering faith?

Where do you see God allowing Satan to test you as Job was tested? How have you responded?

7

Military Journey Ends and Civilian Life Begins

For the LORD giveth wisdom: out of his mouth cometh knowledge and understanding.

Prov 2:6 KJV

When I got out the military in 1995 there was a program being offered to those who were in for a certain period of time and wanted to get out. I decided to apply for the program not knowing what was ahead. I felt the time was right. As in all my decisions, I laid it out before God and asked for guidance on the direction I should take. Sometimes we have these life changing decisions to make and we're not sure how to approach them, remember Matthew 7:7-8, we have to put these things into action. We often recite scriptures and never put them into practice.

I decided not to get a job with the military because I wanted to know how to be a civilian and live among them. I applied for many jobs, including one at a hospital in the area. I really did not know what I wanted to do, I just applied for all the jobs I thought I could do.

I started off as a part-time medical clerk in one of the departments. As time went on, I decided that I wanted a full-time position, but none were available in that department. I told my supervisor that I needed something full-time, so she made arrangements with the emergency room department for me to work there on my days off.

I don't think that there was anyone else who had worked two part-time positions in the same company. While working in the ER I encountered patients who were badly hurt, and I had to go and talk to them while they were being worked on. I did not do very well with the sight of blood, being as squeamish as I was I did not handle working in the emergency room very well. I was good when the day passed without any trauma.

I experienced folks grieving because their loved one had passed away. I was a mess when that happened, but I would try so hard to hold my tears back in order to be of service to them. One day they brought in a patient who was in a car accident, I was supposed to go in and get his information and the person training me told me what to ask. I got to the door and told her that I was not able to do it and she just went in and bent over him and asked, "what's your name?" Then and there I knew I could not work in the ER.

I finally decided that I could not handle this setting any longer. I started looking for another full-time position. I found a position as a clerk in another department. With that position, I thought that I was capable of much more. One day I was looking on the job board and one of the ladies in a supervisory position saw me looking and asked what I was doing. I told her I needed something else. She asked if I had a degree and I said no. She asked if I was in college and I told her I was. At the time I was working on my General Studies degree. She asked for a copy of my transcript. I was nervous because I was not sure what she was going to do.

I was given a position that required a degree, that required me knowing much more than I did at the time.

Remember, He will always take care of you and He will at times place you among Kings and Queens and give you the tools you need to accomplish the task. I had to fall back on my military training because my very first assignment was to review paper charts, collect the data so that it could be analyzed by a statistician and the findings shared with visiting members from The World Health Organization WHO. My training kicked in when I walked in the door of the clinic with my supervisor and another coworker who were there before me, and they asked me, "what do we need to do?" My stomach dropped at that moment and I had to ask God to help me. Here I am supposed to be getting trained and I am being asked what to do. I figured it was a test at the time and I needed to prove myself.

I am reminded of Joseph who rose up to be great even with his background as a slave. Yes, I had to work hard and at times without the guidance of others, but I knew the God I trusted in would not let me down. And if He did it for me, He can and will do it for you. He will place you in positions where His certification is all you need. Trust Him when He does that.

Have you ever experienced Him elevating you when you thought you were not qualified?

8

People God Sends as Answered Prayer

"...A man was going down from Jerusalem to Jericho, when he was attacked by robbers. They stripped him of his clothes, beat him and went away, leaving him half dead. A priest happened to be going down the same road, and when he saw the man, he passed by on the other side. So too, a Levite, when he came to the place and saw him, passed by on the other side. But a Samaritan, as he traveled, came where the man was; and when he saw him, he took pity on him. He went to him and bandaged his wounds, pouring on oil and wine. Then he put the man on his own donkey, brought him to an inn and took care of him. The next day he took out two denarii and gave them to the innkeeper. 'Look after him,' he said, 'and when I return, I will reimburse you for any extra expense you may have.' "Which of these three do you think was a neighbor to the man who fell into the hands of robbers?" The expert in the law replied, "The

> *one who had mercy on him." Jesus told him, "Go and do*
> *likewise."*
>
> *Luke 10:30-37 NIV*

While in the military I met my best friend, an older sister, a blessing to me and my family. She was trying to get some paperwork done and was a bit upset because she was not getting the help she needed. She came into my office upset that day and I asked if I could help. I helped her get her paperwork submitted. Her request was approved and from there we became great friends. I was adopted into her family and was invited to all family gatherings. As our friendship grew I found out she had issues with her teenage daughter. Those issues were similar to the ones I was experiencing. Because of this she knew how to help me.

God knew what was ahead for me and He placed this person in my life who had been through the same things that I was about to experience in my life. She was with me when I was having issues with my daughter running away from home at 3:00AM and many other times after that. We are now family, and we are there for each other. She is still there for me and I thank God for placing her in my life.

My oldest daughter was about seventeen years old and constantly running away from home. She was rebellious and did not want to follow my instructions. This experience shook me to the core because I thought I was a good mother and should not be going through something like this. My faith at the time was shaken. I would beat myself up saying, maybe I was not a good mother. I would call my mother and talk to her and she reminded me that I did the best I could do. I went and looked for her time and time again, but when I got her home she would leave again. Frustrated and not sure what else to do, I prayed for help and asked God to send it soon. A soldier, years older (in his 30s) saw her walking the streets and took her in. This soldier lived downtown and I had never met him before.

For a couple days I wrestled with it because he was much older than she was but started looking at what I had asked God for. I kept saying to myself, I prayed for help and God sent the help. Who am I to question how the help came?

Sometimes, when we ask God to help us, He uses the most unlikely people or things to answer our request and if we do not pay attention, we will miss our answered prayer. We can't assume that God is thinking like us, because He does not. He could use your enemy to answer your prayer. We need to be aware of what He is doing in our lives when we send out our request hoping for an answer. I try to pay attention to my questions and His answers, because He is always there in my time of need.

After a while I got the courage to meet the young man, and from my understanding there was nothing romantic going on at the beginning. He took care of her for over a year and she was stable during that time. I knew where she was and that she was doing fine. He then got orders to go to Korea and left her with his apartment and his furniture. While in Korea he called and asked me for permission to marry her. I did give him permission, but while he was gone, she became rebellious again and with child. I was back to having my faith tested. During this period, I was trying to get her to graduate from school. I had placed her in an alternative school that helps students graduate. Some days I would get calls from the Principal telling me that she was threatening to leave the school. Then I would jump in the car and speed down the highway, 90 miles an hour to get there and make sure she did not leave. With a whole lot of fussing and praying I got there safely, and they managed to keep her there until I got there. After much perseverance and prayer, we finally got her across the stage at about five months pregnant.

Are you rejecting the help that God sends you because it is unconventional?

9

He Prepared a Table Before Me

[When King David's son Absalom starts a coup, a humiliated King David is forced to flee Jerusalem in exile. After days of traveling in the harsh wilderness with little provision, he and his companions] camped in the land of Gilead. When David came to Mahanaim, Shobi son of Nahash from Rabbah of the Ammonites, and Makir son of Ammiel from Lo Debar, and Barzillai the Gileadite from Rogelim brought bedding and bowls and articles of pottery. They also brought wheat and barley, flour and roasted grain, beans and lentils, honey and curds, sheep, and cheese from cows' milk for David and his people to eat. For they said, "The people have become exhausted and hungry and thirsty in the wilderness."

2 Samuel 17:26-29 NIV

Thanksgiving and the holiday season were fast approaching and I was trying my hardest not to be upset by the lack of splendor the season would bring. My funds were low, and things were looking mighty slim for my family. I did not have anything to cook a decent Thanksgiving meal with. I was planning on just having a regular day without all the trimmings that go into having a great Thanksgiving. We were just sitting around, when to our surprise the doorbell rang (I think about a week or so before) and there stood a few people from a church, miles away from where I live. We were not sure why they were there, and when they told me that they were there to deliver provisions to us. I could not believe it. I am not sure how these folks got my information, but who is questioning God? They had one large tub and a small one of groceries, everything to prepare a thanksgiving meal and much more. I could not help but shed tears of joy and gratitude.

After being thankful for what God had provided, I thought that was it. But God had covered us for the whole season. The same group came back at Christmas and brought lots of clothes and toys for the children. The children were very excited that they had all those toys. Now I really cried. God takes care of me in spite of my faults. If He can do it for me, He can do it for you. That was one of the best Christmas holidays we ever had.

Will you trust Him to answer your prayers and fulfill all your needs?

What wilderness are you crossing that you need to trust in God to provide?

10

Paid the Debt

*And my God will meet all your needs according to the riches
of his glory in Christ Jesus.*

Philippians 4:19 NIV

As you know, we often times get ourselves in debt and
sometimes it seems there is no end in sight as to how
to get out. I had a bill from Beneficial that had become
somewhat of a ball and chain around my neck. I knew that
if I got rid of it, things would be much easier to handle. I
started praying for help.

One Sunday morning, I was ironing the kid's clothes for
church and decided to ask God out loud for help to get rid
of that bill.

We went to church and the choir was singing. The lady
who was the soloist began giving her testimony about how
she had adopted her grandkids and how God had blessed
her with some money. I too did adopt kids. I was in
amazement of the amount she mentioned. I quickly pulled
out a piece of paper and wrote my name and phone

number down and decided to find this lady after church. I did not find her but did give my information to the Choir Director to pass on to her.

For a while I did not hear from her, then one day the phone finally rang. She said that she was a CPA and would help me with what needed to be done. I also received help from the IRS to finalize the documents. The process took a year, but it was worth the wait. When everything was finalized, I was able to pay off a $19,000.00 bill. Now that was God!

Do you have a major request you need to trust God to help you with?

11

The Adoption

Speak up for those who cannot speak for themselves,
for the rights of all who are destitute.
Speak up and judge fairly; defend the rights of the poor
and needy.

Proverbs 31:8-9 NIV

I became a grandmother at the ripe age of 38. I was devastated that I was going to be a grandmother at that age. I had often thought that grandmothers were old folks and now here I am inducted into the club. My daughter ended up having four children within the period of seven years. She was often struggling with them and I had to step in to help. I kept them on and off through the years. One afternoon I got a call from her neighbor stating that she had tried to kill herself by taking a bunch of pills and that the ambulance was there and I needed to come and get the children. The children were in the house when she attempted to overdose. She was also pregnant at the time of the attempt.

When I arrived, I saw her as the medics were placing her in the ambulance. I got the kids from the house and asked the neighbor to call Child Protective Services (CPS) and let them know what had happened and that the children were with me. I was in for a long night. In the midst of the crisis I prayed and asked God to take control of the situation because I was not sure how I was going to handle it. I had to go to the hospital to see how she was doing and also met with CPS there. It was well after midnight when we left the hospital and CPS came to inspect my home to see if it was safe for the children to be there.

Now the long process had started with numerous visits from CPS, classes and other related mandatory functions. While going through this, I was having issues at work due to the time I had to take off, taking care of the kids and meeting with CPS. In a few months I was expecting my daughter to give birth and I had to take that baby also. What was I going to do? I had raised three kids and was about to take on a newborn. All I could do was ask God for the strength to take care of all three kids. My granddaughter was born, and I took her straight from the hospital home. My job did not want to give me the time off to take care of her. It was a struggle because the baby had jaundice and was admitted to the hospital a few times for breathing issues.

God was working things out. Yes, I cried, I called my mom and asked her how did I do it the first time around? Starting over with three kids was not easy. My mom and sister came from New York and Dallas to help me out and that relieved some of my stress. After using up my vacation time I had to return to work. My granddaughter was too young to go to daycare. Six weeks was when they are able to be in daycare. The other two children were in daycare and I had to talk to the owner to see if she would take a four-week old. She agreed to help me out after I explained my work situation.

God provided me with some of the most compassionate CPS workers. I would often hear horror stories about CPS, but that was not my experience. They walked me through the whole process. Each step required a new worker. For two years I was back and forth to court. They were trying to see if my daughter was fit enough to take the kids, but that was not the case. I finally went through the adoption process in 2009. I realized all the tears that I shed, and all the sleepless nights would be over because they were growing fast and before I knew it the baby was in pre-K and I could breath. Today the baby is a tall beautiful eleven-year old and each year she has a birthday I shed a tear because I see how far God has brought me. The oldest recently graduated from high school and yes, I had a full heart for how far I came and the blessings along the way.

Were there times in your life when you were struggling and thought that there was no help in sight?

12

The Move

For I know the plans I have for you, declares the LORD, plans for welfare and not for evil, to give you a future and a hope.

Jeremiah 29:11 ESV

For years my family had been asking me to move from Texas to Las Vegas, but I did not feel the urge to do so. I made a visit during Christmas in 2017 for two weeks. While visiting I was having a good feeling of being around family and being there to help my father. Upon my return to Texas, I decided that I was going to take the challenge and put things in motion for the move. I had various conversations with God and asked for His guidance with the move.

I started getting rid of things I would no longer need, some things that moved with me since I first joined the military. I even had boxes that still were unpacked from my previous move to Texas 25 years earlier. These small steps were my working in faith. I called the bank to get some realtor referrals. I was connected to an awesome realtor. He walked me through the whole process, and he had a variety of outlets to showcase my home. We decided to list my home in February thinking that it would take a while to sell. I did all the necessary things needed to prepare for showings. He photographed the home and posted it online.

The home went live online on a Friday and on Saturday I had a showing scheduled. I went around the home praying and asking God to work things out for me. So right before leaving the home so that the prospective buyer could see it, I turned and said, "God do Your thing". God did what I asked, the person who viewed the home made an offer and with that offer that meant that I had to move in March. I was in shock and became nervous and anxious. Yes, I trust God and have faith that He answers prayers but did not expect it to be that fast. I was going off what I had seen in the neighborhood, houses were up for a very long time, so I was working from what I had seen. (I think God was having a good time seeing me go into shock from His move. I guess He was saying, "you asked").

I started feeling the stress of a sudden move and ended up in the hospital. I had to go back to God and be specific in my request. My children were still in school and I wanted them to finish school before the move so that they could start fresh. I prayed and asked Him to allow them to finish out the school year. The person who had made the offer then changed their mind due to them having another home and they could not handle two mortgages. I then exhaled and breathed a little easier. As time went by, there were numerous people in and out of the home to view it and no offers. Time was winding down and the kids were getting ready to get out of school.

I started wondering about when I would get another offer. In the meantime, I scheduled the movers (not knowing what the outcome would be). I did not want to have a house payment after I moved, so I kept on talking to God. I told Him that I knew He was working on my request, but I was getting nervous that I had no buyer. I bought a plane ticket for a certain day in faith. I could not get any refunds if I changed it.

Finally, I had one person scheduled after a while of not having anyone walking through. I did my usual walk through and left early just in case the scheduled person would show up early. I had security cameras in the home and knew when someone entered the home. As soon as I left, someone entered. I was stunned, because they were really early. I looked through the cameras and saw them walk through and then something happened. As I was watching I saw what looked like the realtor for them throw her hands in the air in a manner of praising God. I was trying to understand what had just happened. When they left, I decided to wait to see if the person who had a scheduled time to be there would show. The scheduled person showed, did their walkthrough and left. I later received an offer and that offer came from the folks who were not scheduled to be there. Yes, the unscheduled person bought my home. God is so awesome. The movers came and packed us up two days before the kids got out of school and picked up the furniture a day after they got out of school. Cleaners showed, inspectors did their inspection, and everything was moving without a hitch. I had scheduled my car to be picked up a couple days prior to me flying out, that was done during the scheduling of the movers when I did not know how things would work out. God worked it all out.

While I was preparing for the move from Texas to Las Vegas, I was also working with a realtor in Las Vegas. I was looking at homes online and placing my bids as I saw something I liked. One day I received a link for a home and when I looked at it, I became really emotional. It looked like something you saw in a magazine. I started asking God if I deserved something like that. I showed the link to my best friend whom I was staying with and she said, "let's pray about it". We prayed that God would work it out and if the home was to be mine, it would be.

I placed my bid and waited. The next day I was told that someone had outbid me. I chalked it up to, it was not intended to be mine. I continued to put in offers on other homes and still nothing. Once I made it to Las Vegas, I waited to see if any of my offers were accepted, but nothing. My sister took me to look at some homes that were being built. I did like them, but they wanted quite a bit of money down. I then said to myself, if I do not get an offer accepted by the next Tuesday/Wednesday I was going to talk to the builders even though that was not what I really wanted. In the meantime, I was asking God to work things out.

That Tuesday the realtor texted me and said, "you know the house you REALLY liked, it is back on the market".

I was not sure which one he was talking about since I had placed bids on quite a few homes. He sent the link and I could not believe that the same house I had prayed about was the very same one in the link. He asked if I wanted to resubmit my bid. I resubmitted my bid and it was accepted. I was so overwhelmed at how God worked it all out. Every time I talk about it, I get emotional. My God is a GREAT God!

The children got into a good school and for the first time I was involved at their school. There were events that took place prior to the move that were also tied into the move. The April before I took my car for an oil change. I got the oil change and went home. After getting home I received a call from the dealer that they had forgotten to do something on my car and if I could bring it back for them to finish it up. I took it back and while they were working on my car, I was walking the lot checking out the latest and greatest. I looked at two cars, but this one particular car caught my eye. The salesman came out and I told him that I was only looking. He said that was ok, but if I wanted, I could test drive either one. I kept walking between the two cars and it just seemed like one was calling my name (smile). I test drove it and then decided I was going to get it. How do you go from getting an oil change to buying a new car? I bought the car, they credited the oil change to the new car. I did not know how many bells and whistles I had included in the purchase. I went home, went to work, and continued my normal day to day routine.

Four months later I was let go from my job. I cannot say that I was worried, because I had prayed about me leaving the job, as I was no longer feeling enthusiastic about the job. The stress was very high, and I wanted out. When I was let go, I was escorted to the door and I told the person who escorted me that God was in control. Oh, by the way, I scheduled my own firing. I had made an appointment to see "the boss". When I showed up I was greeted by her and HR. I asked if I was in trouble and was told no. I was told that my position was done away with. I calmly handed in my badge and went to get my things from the office. A few months before that, I had cleared out my office and took my things home.

I was given the option to find something else in the institution, but every time I got a call and it was their number, I started having anxiety attacks. Someone I knew there called me one day and said that he had a position if I wanted it. I told him that I really did not want to go back to that institution, 22 years was enough. Once I had that out there, I stopped having anxiety attacks when their number showed on my phone.

I was at home, with no job and was awfully calm about it. I had my conversations with God and asked Him to work things out for me. After selling my home, I paid off my car. Looking at it now, I needed a good working car to get the kids back and forth to school now that they didn't have a school bus for the new school. From the bells and whistles, my oil changes are paid for a while. Having three kids in school, it can be a bit expensive. They wear uniforms to school and their meals are paid for.

My son got accepted into a local college that will pay for two years, so when he graduates from high school he will start there. During this time, whenever I had any doubts I would get woken up in the middle of the night with scriptures, scriptures like Psalm 27:14. This happened numerous times and it would be at 3:00 or 4:00 AM. Now that I am in a new place, I am awaiting what mission God has for me. I am patiently waiting for ALL the great things He has in store for me.

Was there ever a time in your life when God moved in such a way that even though you trust Him, you were still so amazed by Him coming through for you?

13

A Whole Lot of God Moments

While going through on the job, I got a call from another department asking me if I needed a job. Without hesitation, I said yes. There was God.

The baby was sickly and had to be hospitalized a couple of times and my new department was very understanding. They even helped in getting doctor's appointments when I was told there were no available appointments left. There was God.

My previous boss decided not to give me a raise from my evaluation, but when I went to the new department, I was given one, one that I did not expect. Nothing but God.

During the time of me taking on the new baby, He sent me case workers who looked out for me and walked me through the process of their system. Every step of the way, there was God. There were days when I had no energy, I was so depleted that I felt like quitting, but there was God.

I was having a hard time at work and my stress was mounting. I started looking for jobs but could not find one. If you have been through situations like this, you know how depressing and stressful it can be. I knew I had done nothing wrong, and when I work, I try to do it as unto God. I had to write down every single thing I did during the course of the day. When I showed it to the boss, he said "I did not know you did this much." I thought that when he asked that question I was free and clear, but it continued. I started asking God for help.

A Catholic friend of mine gave me some holy water and I went in early one morning and just started praying and anointing my cube with the holy water. I got so frustrated I had to go talk to someone about the situation. With that said, I went to a mail-stop to conduct business. While standing in line I noticed they had a magnet rack and saw one magnet among the pool of magnets that said, "Grow where God plants You." On a regular day, you would have to walk up to the stand to see what the inscription said. Needless to say, I bought it to remind me that in spite of what I was going through I had a mission to be an example to the people I worked with. Through the years while going through stress, I have prayed with many and counseled many.

Are you going through a situation that you need to grow where He plants you?

How are you handling it?

Epilogue

Keeping the Faith

I can do all things through Christ which strengtheneth me.

Philippians 4:13 KJV

With the way the world is today, it is often difficult to keep the faith. So many distractions happen to make us doubt what God can do. I encourage you to keep your eyes fixed on God and know that whatever the situation, whatever the problem, He is there for you. We need to practice trusting God so that when we face the storms of life, we are well-equipped to go through them. In keeping the faith, we need to also know that sometimes things won't go our way. When that happens, we need to ask God about the lesson in the disappointments we face. Yes, we will be disappointed, we will be sad, we will have pain, but just know that God will bring you through it all.

As you can see over the years, I have been through many moments where I had to call on my Heavenly Father to bring me out. Those moments were not always exciting, but when I look back and see all the "but God" moments, I can do nothing but praise God for those moments. I happen to come out stronger than I was before each moment. It may not seem that He is strengthening you during this time, but in time you will realize that He is. It may take weeks, months, or even years for you to realize how much stronger you are after that. I know that I am. I encourage you to stay the course and don't give up.

About the Author

Anne Marie Scott was born in Linstead, St. Catherine, Jamaica where her faith journey began. She grew up in the Newlands Foursquare church where she gained her foundation of faith. She migrated to the United States in 1979 where she later joined the military and served fourteen years honorably. She is a mother of three grown children and grandmother of four; raising three of the four. Being a parent in the military was at times difficult, because she had to deploy to distant countries and leave the children behind to be cared for by someone else. Becoming a grandparent at an early age was life changing for her. Nonetheless, she picked up the mantle and learned. She is also a Gulf war Veteran and now resides in Las Vegas.